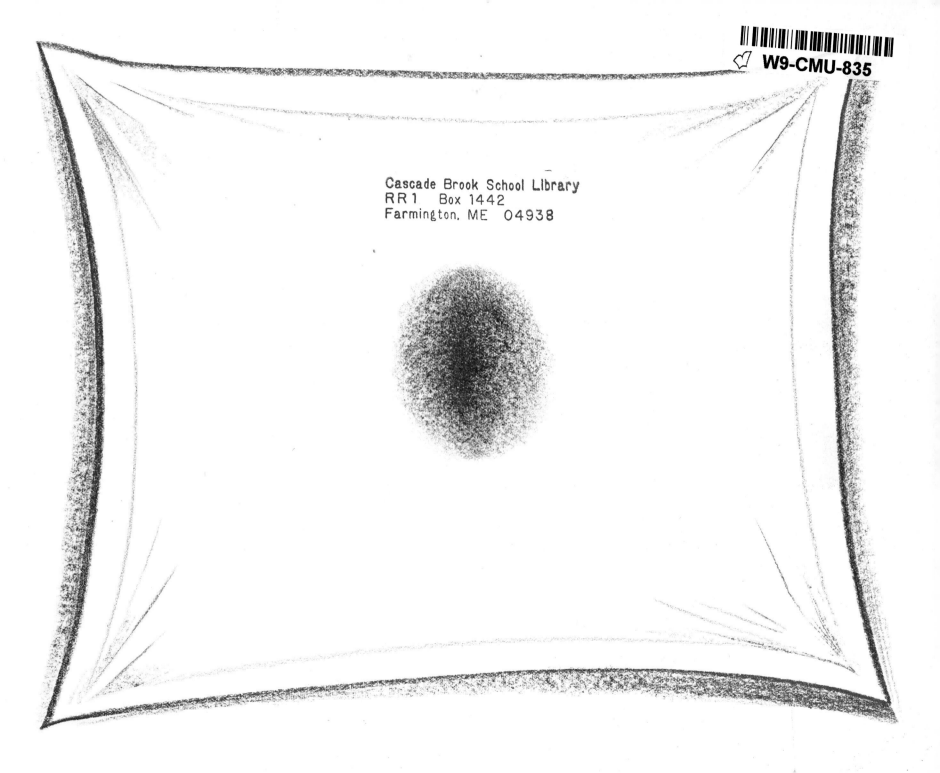

Cascade Brook School Library
RR 1   Box 1442
Farmington, ME   04938

DYING TO SMOKE

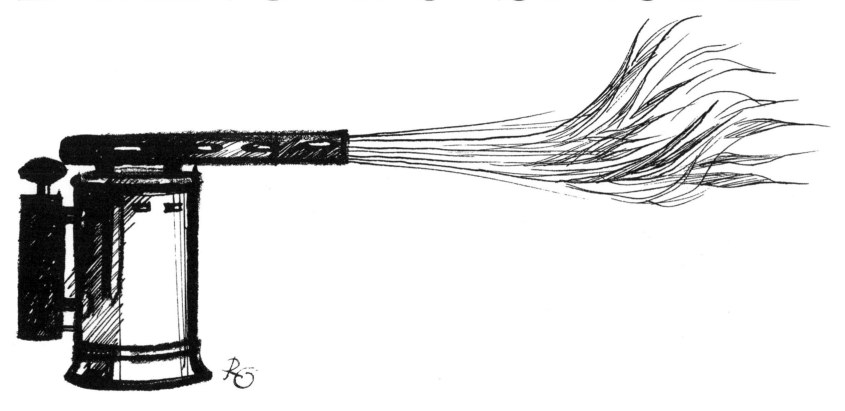

by Robert Osborn and Fred W. Benton, M.D.

HOUGHTON MIFFLIN COMPANY BOSTON

Library of Congress Catalog Card Number: 64-15836

ISBN: 0-395-08058-4

FIFTH PRINTING W

He's afire!

Burning dried leaves

was something Sir Walter Raleigh

learned from the savages.

Burning smoke into you

           can be a dizzy-making early delight.

It would be silly to deny the fact.

Because you feel you're out there

really swinging;

YOU are in charge now.

You're rebelling if you want to.

You feel you look like an . . .

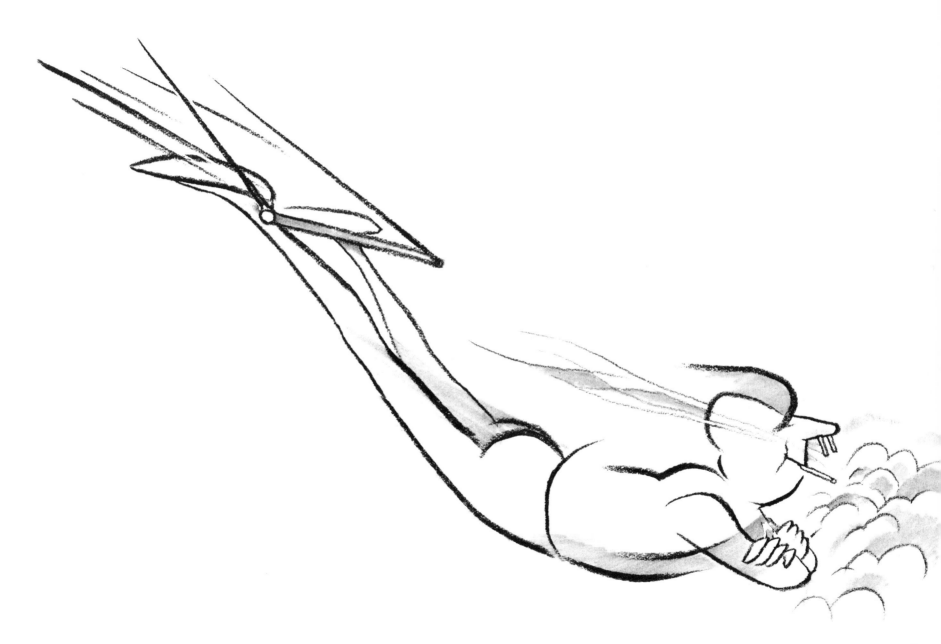

adult.

11

For <u>various</u> reasons

some people

slide into smoking.

There are a lot of social and physical pressures which may force you into it

and even though you

are lighting them back-

ward and forward and getting

smoke in your eyes and

browning your fingers . . . you feel they

confer sophistication . . . also they are becoming HABITUAL.

You've probably even noticed

that there is _considerable_ PRESSURE

being exerted to get

YOU started smoking . . .

EARLY . . .

just like Dad, poor Dad, did.

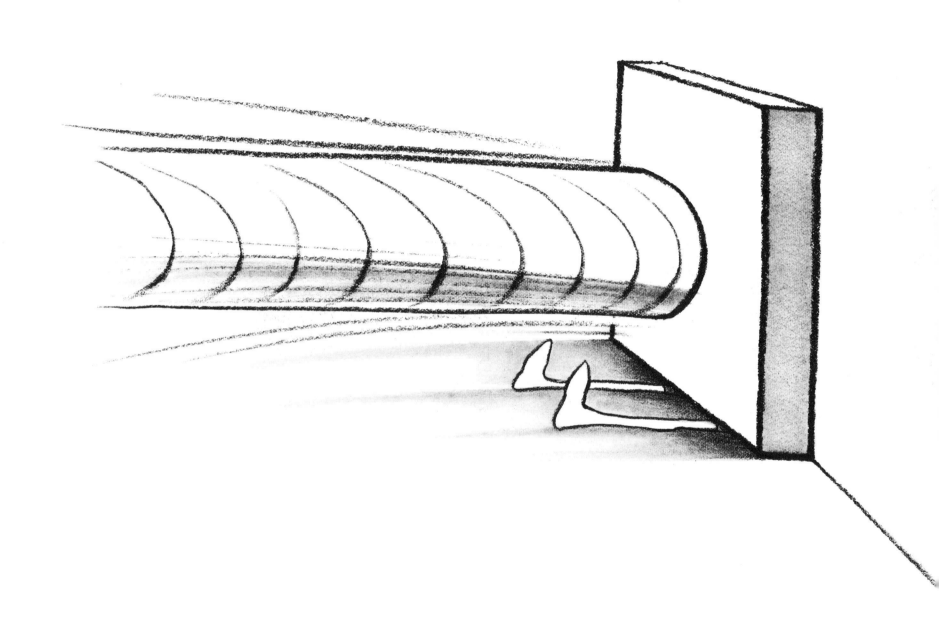

17

In fact last year

207 MILLION dollars

were spent on TV, radio, newspaper and magazine

HARD sell

simply to get YOU to start.

The American Cancer Society used

100 THOUSAND dollars to say the hard facts

(that all DOCTORS now KNOW) about smoking.

19

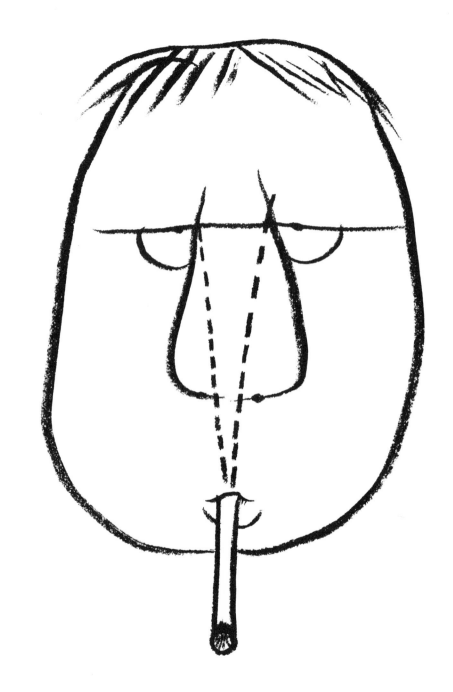

"Well what's wrong with all this?

It's a free country isn't it?"

Nothing's wrong . . .

EXCEPT...

Somehow you are not being informed

that death from all causes DECREASED rapidly

in the past 50 years.

BUT death from one disease connected with inhalation

INcreased 600% in men . . . 125% in women.

Also you aren't told what inhaling does

to the circulation of blood through your lungs,

heart, and blood vessels.

It's probably too unpleasant a thought!

how's
that
again ?

23

4000 of you are starting every day . . .

repeat, 4000 **new** starting smokers

EVERY day!

and once **STARTED**

you are

on the way

to being

. . . HOOKED.

I must make all the others look like "retards"

I cough but I can still bear it!

I can see what they meant about habit forming!

27

And let's face it—

as far as smoking and hot tars go

it's obvious that WE're **NOT**

made of glazed brick!

WE're **NOT** fire resistant!

WE're **NOT** chimneys!

Instead, we're made of the most

delicate WET cells and tissue.

We can SMOKE hams, BROIL steaks,

and even PICKLE calves' feet;

but, if we smoke our own bodies

we're inviting four diseases . . .

any one of which may KILL us

. . . and inviting is no word for it!

There will be those STURDY souls

who pile on the protective armor . . .

who won't admit the truth

I don't care
WHAT the
facts are!

35

even though

      ENGLISH doctors

      WEST GERMAN doctors

      RUSSIAN doctors

      SWEDISH doctors

      DANISH doctors

      (and American doctors, finally . . .)

are backing the compiled and published damaging facts

about smoking.

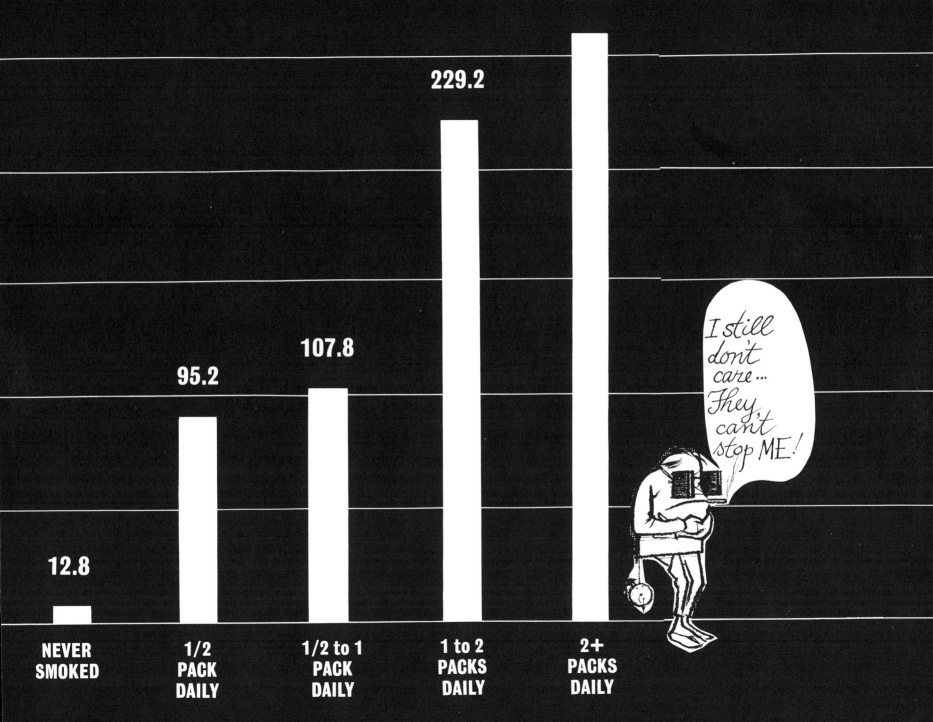

IMAGINATION is the key!

With it you'll SEE what the next pages mean to YOU,

and how and why they affect you . . .

and finally what YOU can do.

WITHOUT IMAGINATION you won't

even sense the error of ever starting

and the exacerbation of withdrawal!

These pages are not pretty but they are what

we now OBSERVE inhaling does to us . . .

and that is all this book is about.

If YOU are a lover of the truth . . .

read on . . .

the facts are unpleasant but they are here.

If you are a self-swindler

you'll put this book away now . . . and cheat.

This surgeon looks within the chest almost every day

and is witness to the appearance, texture, and behavior of the lung.

A worn-out lung cannot be replaced with a new one. When

the lung is destroyed by cancer, its removal may save

the patient's life. Many have a cancer that is surgically

out-of-bounds when the diagnosis is first suspected.

"Why do people talk so much about auto accidents?

Lung cancer kills more people. People should also be

aware that emphysema causes more suffering

and incapacitation than that caused by

all non-fatal accidents."

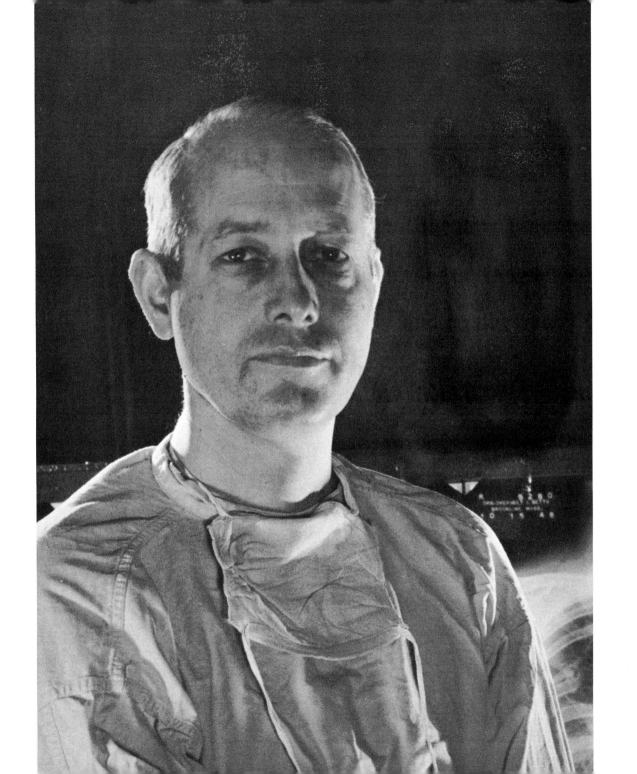

43

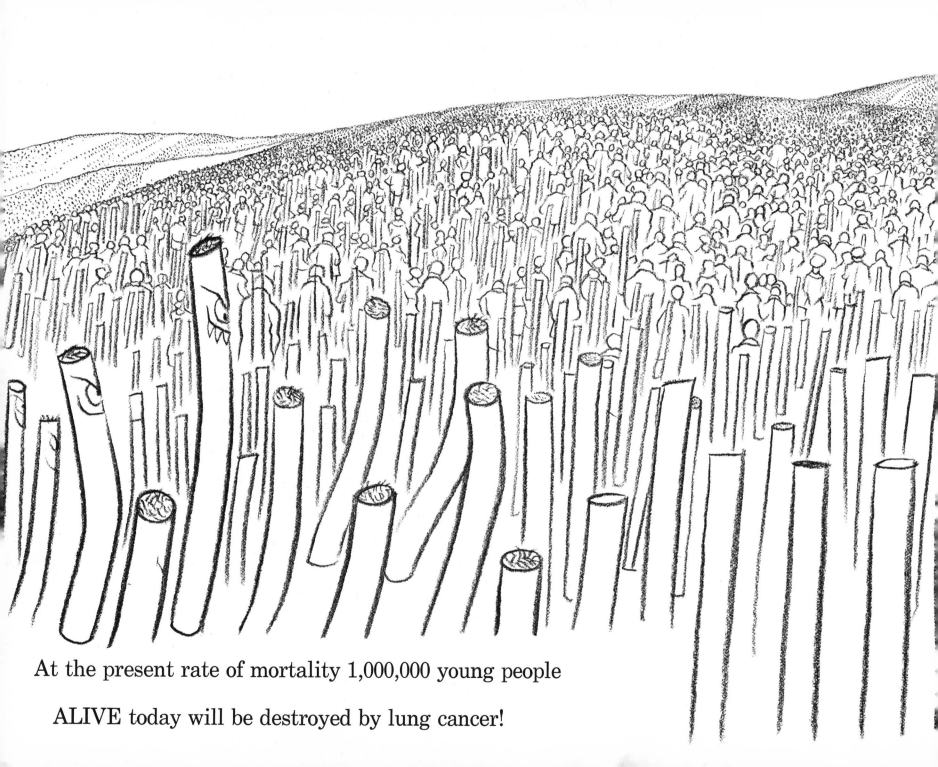

At the present rate of mortality 1,000,000 young people

ALIVE today will be destroyed by lung cancer!

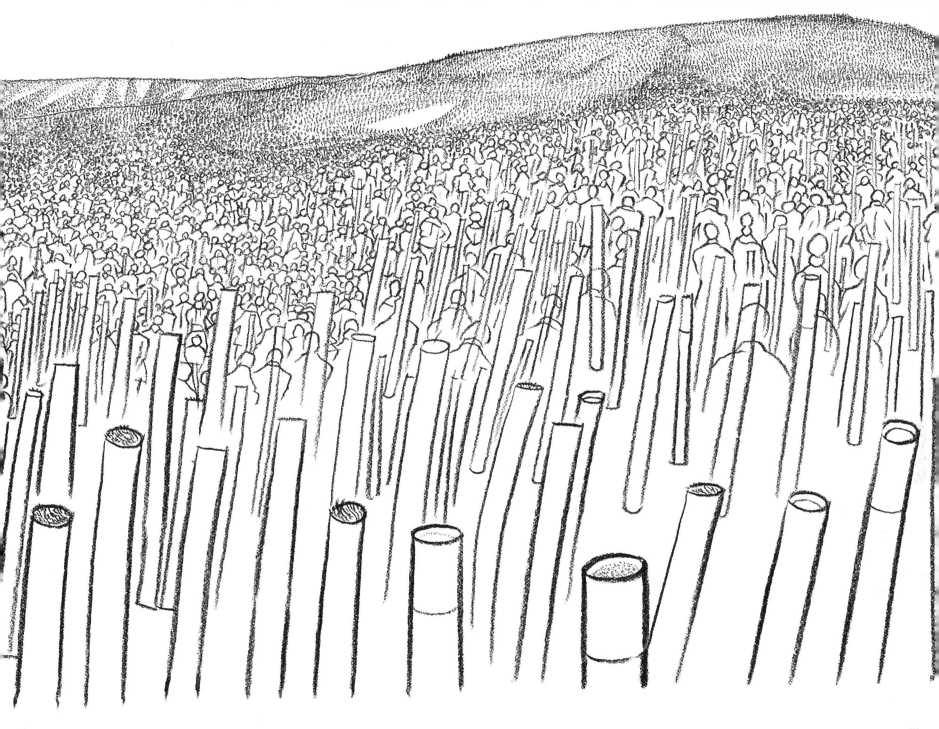

Inhaled smoke not only irritates your mouth and lungs;

it also may make cancers in them.

It hurts your HEART, your stomach,

and in some human beings even their legs.

In women it clearly DAMAGES unborn babies

as evidenced by their lesser weight and premature birth.

Don't try to scare me!

Every time you inhale,

your blood vessels **constrict.**

This is what happens to your blood supply

every time you do it . . .

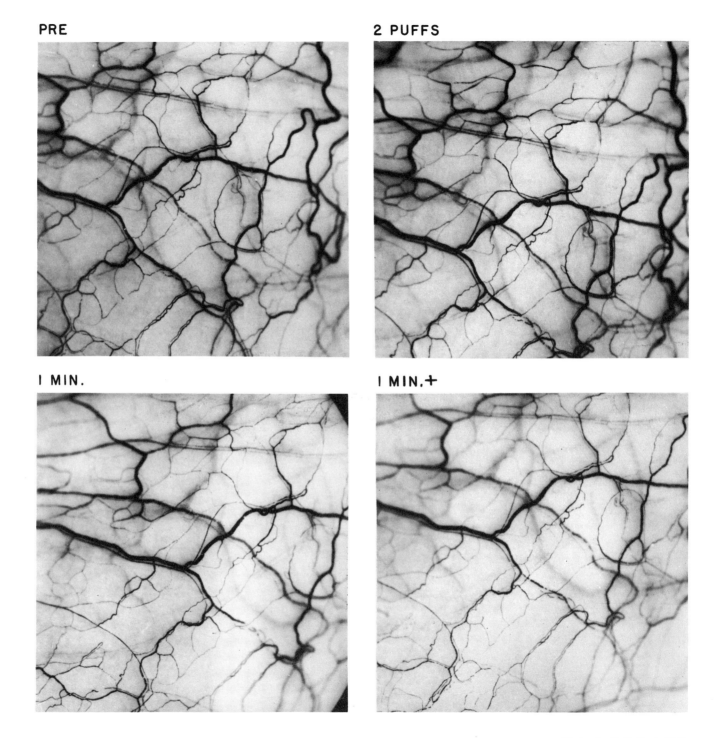

PRE

2 PUFFS

I MIN.

I MIN.+

These are micro-photos of a medical student's small blood vessels.

Photos by S. B. Rees, M.D.

If you keep at it

the damage to the blood vessels

in your lungs and the surrounding air sacs

can be desperately serious . . .

(that is . . . if you love life

Nonsmoker

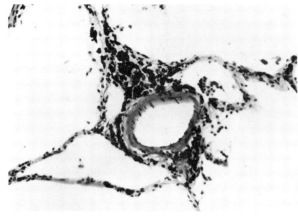

A cross section of a thin-walled, wide-channeled blood vessel surrounded by healthy air sacs.

Moderate smoker

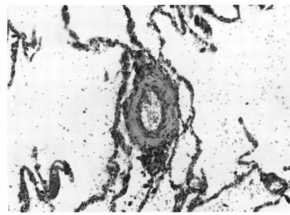

Wall of the blood vessel is somewhat thickened and a few air sacs have ruptured.

Heavy smoker

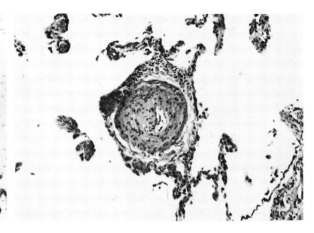

The wall is now so thick the blood channel is nearly closed and almost all walls of the air sacs have ruptured.

and **your** life . . .

Photos courtesy of Dr. Oscar Auerbach
Veterans Administration Hospital, East Orange, N.J.

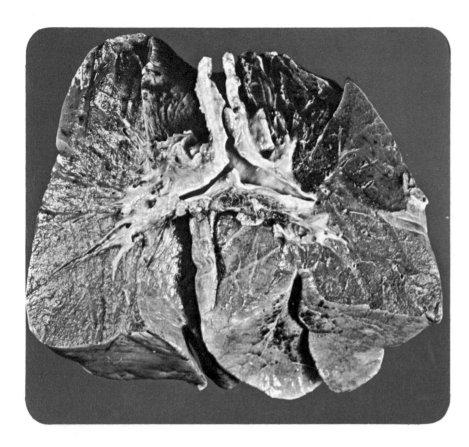

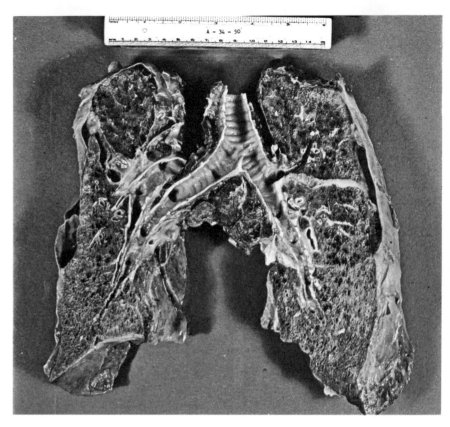

These are the lungs of a nonsmoker (over 60 years of age). Notice that they are not scarred and they inflate well.

These are a smoker's lungs. They are contracted; they are scarred. The air sacs with thickening walls are distended and ruptured in various stages.

This is what EMPHYSEMA is!

Courtesy of Dr. Oscar Auerbach
Veterans Administration Hospital, East Orange, N.J.

SMOKE IRRITATION AND COUGHING

PREPARES THE WAY FOR AND MAY CAUSE

THIS <u>CRIPPLING</u> INJURY TO YOUR LUNGS.

And here's the rub . . .

when the walls of air sacs are **thickened** . . . **distended** . . .

and **ruptured**, the transfer of oxygen to your blood stream

is incomplete. Particularly when the tiny blood vessels

located in the air-sac walls are thickened and obliterated.

If many air sacs and tiny blood vessels are damaged,

the right side of your heart has to <u>beat harder</u> to supply the

<u>pressure</u> to force the same quantity of blood through the remaining

blood vessels. Also, the heart may need to beat faster

to do this. All this <u>increases the work</u> of the heart.

These failures make your heart wear out **<u>early</u>**

gasping for its oxygen . . . trying to get YOU oxygen!

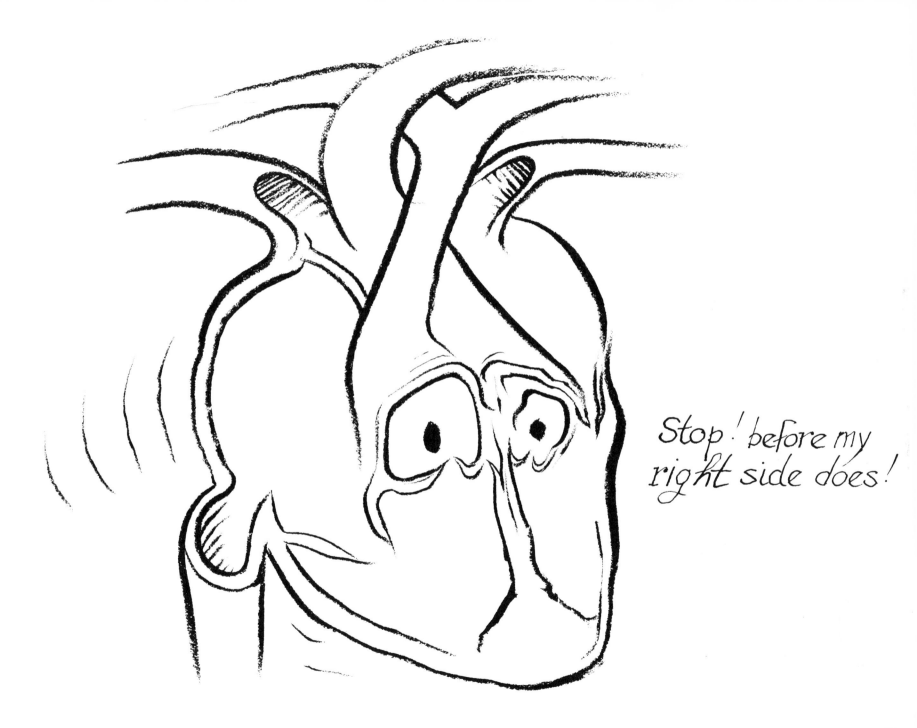

Stop! before my right side does!

No wonder **nearly**

<u>TWICE</u> AS MANY SMOKERS

<u>DIE</u> OF HEART AND CIRCULATORY DISEASES

as nonsmokers.

And the <u>more</u> you inhale the greater your chances

. . . and they are already too great!

Dr. Paul Dudley White, the eminent cardiologist, has said:

"Nicotine tends to raise the blood pressure;

it also increases the WORK of the heart

and it is one of the common causes

of irregularities in the heart beat."

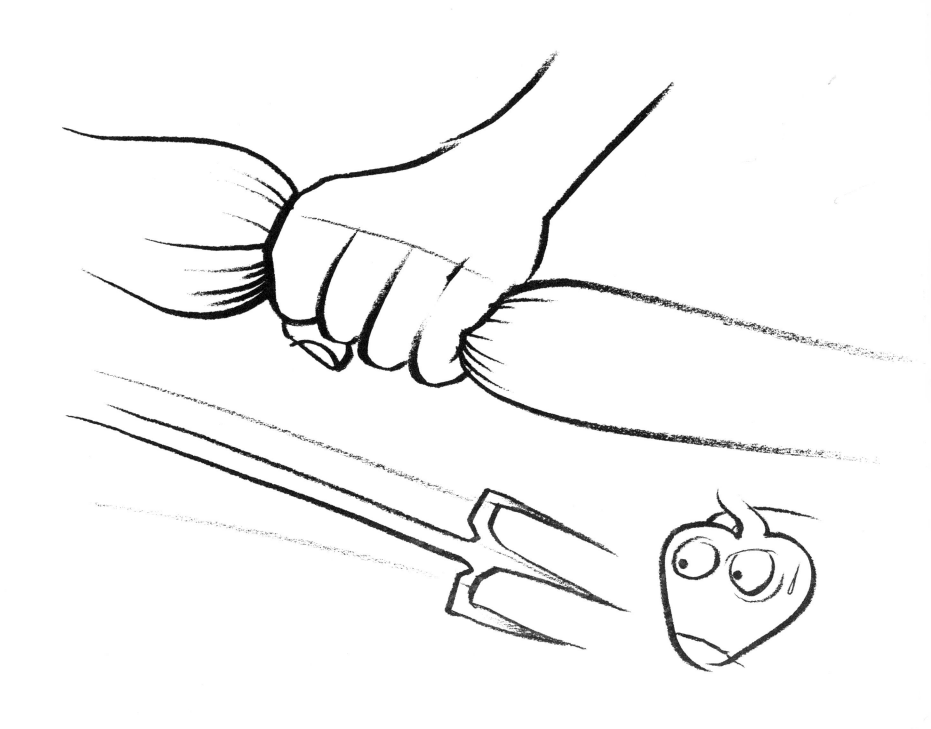

Whether you like it or not, inhaled smoke

contributes to STOMACH ulcers.

Dr. John Ross of Boston's Lahey Clinic says:

"Nicotine stimulates the vagus nerve and in turn

the production of hydrochloric acid in your stomach.

This acid passes out of the stomach

into the duodenum ✠

where most ulcers occur in a susceptible person.

If the protective coating is finally eaten away

an ULCER develops . . .

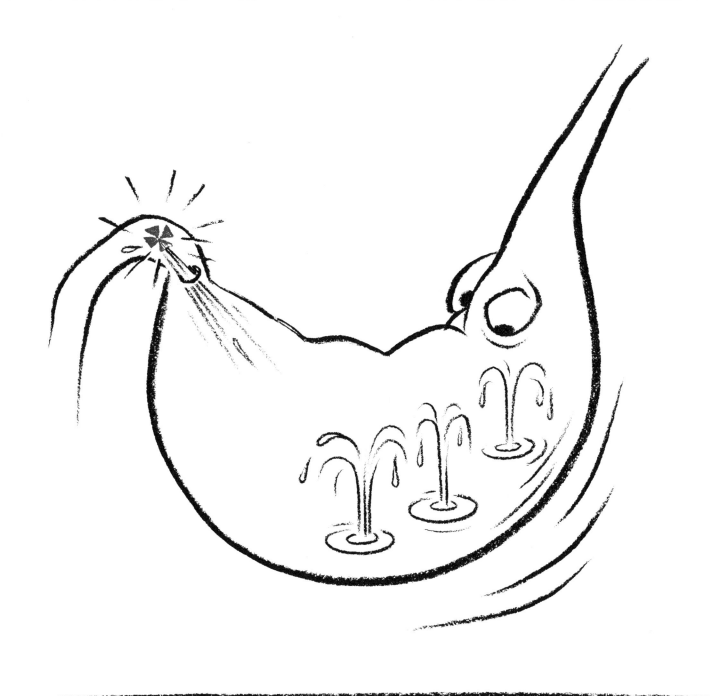

"... and many people who have had an ulcer

will tell you that <u>PAIN</u> INCREASES after inhaling smoke.

AND WORSE ...

that ulcers may not heal

and <u>STAY</u> PROPERLY HEALED

if you continue to smoke."

As for injuring your legs with cigarettes . . .

it's unthinkable . . .

when you're starting.

But in Buerger's disease nicotine constricts the arteries

that carry blood to your legs . . .

with imagined results!

65

Sturdy soul still can't believe any of this . . .

I'm going
to smoke!

67

If you **don't** smoke, the air tubes in your lungs

are lined with beating cilia which move impurities

and mucus UP and out of your lungs.

This happens unconsciously. You don't even sense

that your lungs are being constantly cleared.

INHALED SMOKE PRODUCTS at first SLOW down

the sweeping cilia. And finally

OBLITERATE them entirely.

This is why the confirmed smoker coughs endlessly—

trying to lift the tars, the dust, and the clogging mucus.

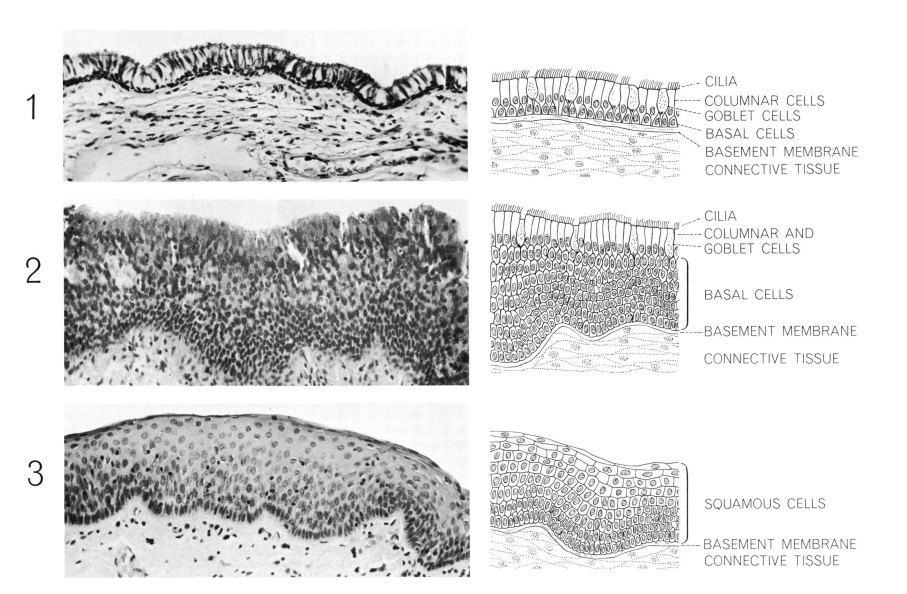

1

CILIA
COLUMNAR CELLS
GOBLET CELLS
BASAL CELLS
BASEMENT MEMBRANE
CONNECTIVE TISSUE

2

CILIA
COLUMNAR AND
GOBLET CELLS

BASAL CELLS

BASEMENT MEMBRANE

CONNECTIVE TISSUE

3

SQUAMOUS CELLS

BASEMENT MEMBRANE
CONNECTIVE TISSUE

Photomicrographs courtesy of Dr. Oscar Auerbach
Drawings courtesy of *Scientific American*. Reprinted with permission.
Copyright © 1962 by Scientific American, Inc. All rights reserved.

Of course none of this is understood at the start . . .

the **easy** start.

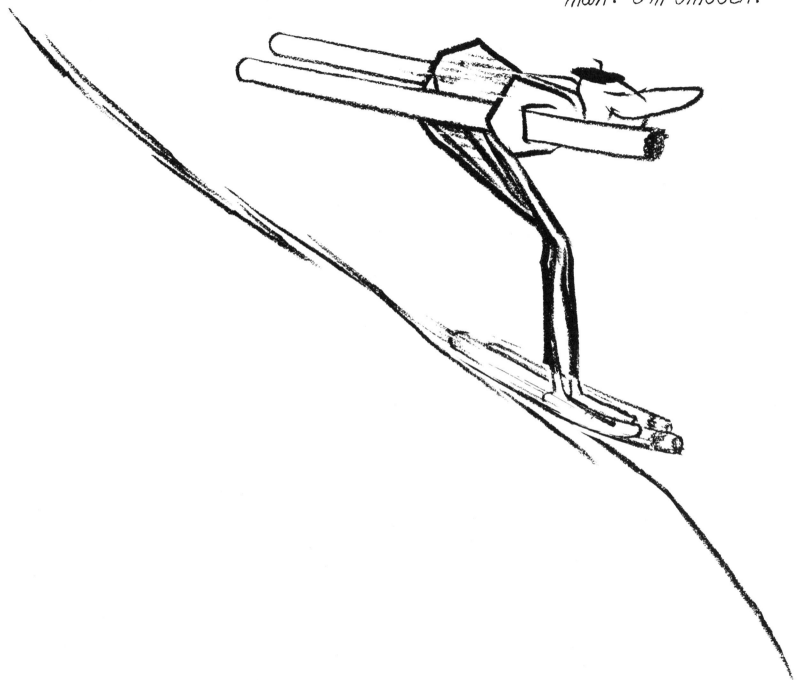

It's when you pick up speed . . .

and are really consuming

the hot tars and nicotine

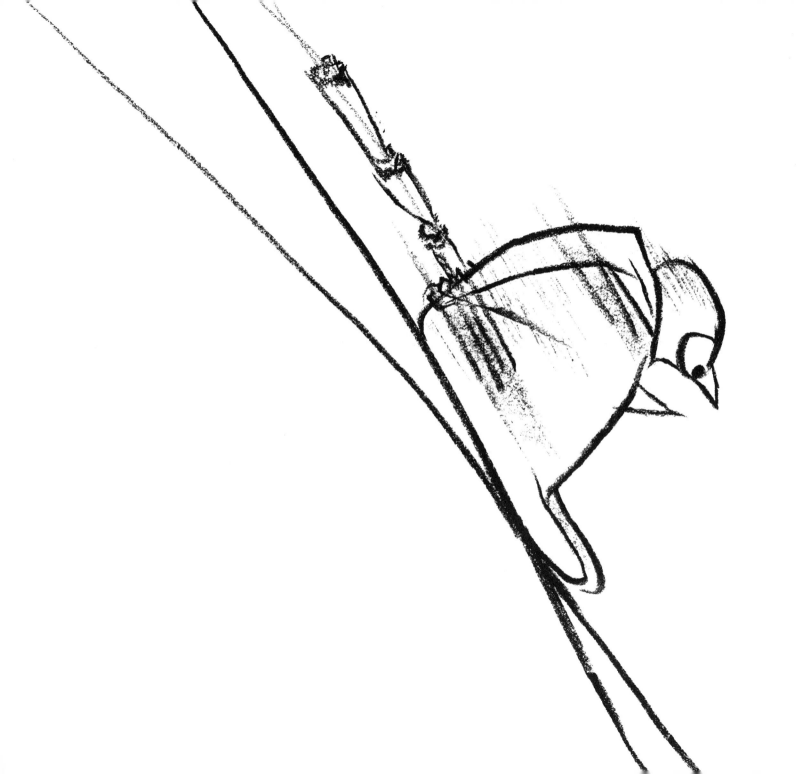

73

that you begin to worry . . .

because you know that you are

out of control and falling free

Why didn't
somebody
warn me?

and you OUGHT to be worried !

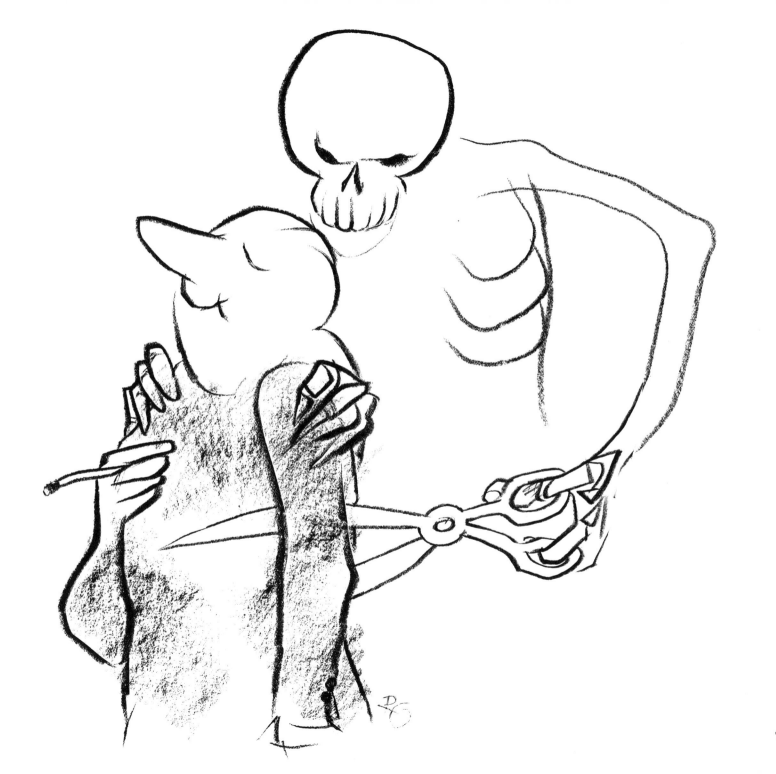

For by now the cilia are being obliterated

in your lungs and this can be followed

by the first appearance of the PRE-cancerous cells

along the air ducts of the lung.

Their nuclei are abnormal;

it is these cells which precede the appearance

of true cancer . . .

4

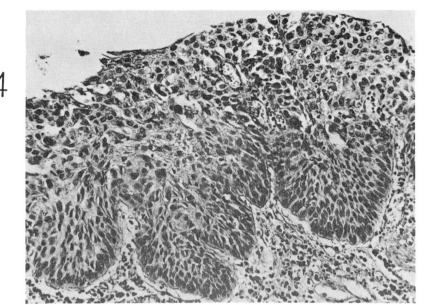

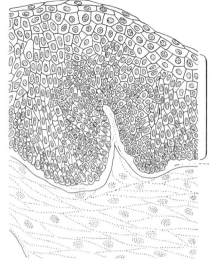

CELLS WITH ATYPICAL NUCLEI

BASEMENT MEMBRANE

CONNECTIVE TISSUE

5

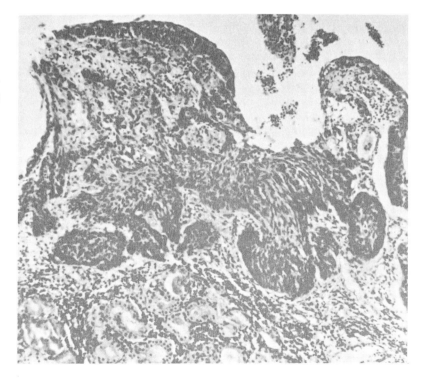

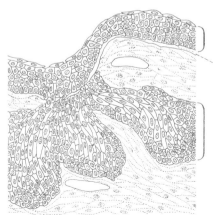

CELLS WITH ATYPICAL NUCLEI

BASEMENT MEMBRANE

EARLY CANCEROUS INVASION

CONNECTIVE TISSUE

This is LUNG CANCER.

This is human lung cancer.

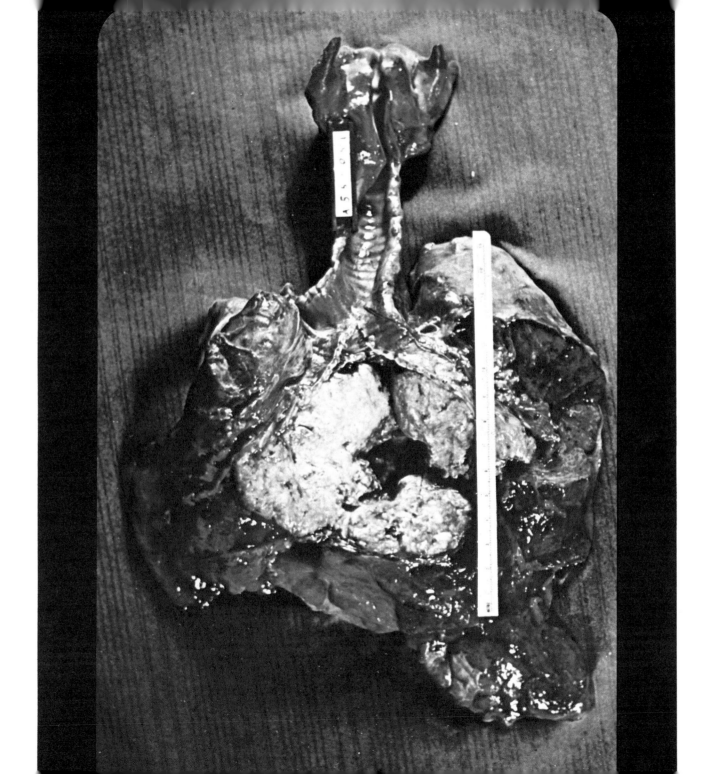

81

And it is this cancer which

in the United States

If present trends

will destroy

is killing <u>more</u> people

than auto accidents . . .

continue it is this cancer which

1,000,000 young people alive today in America.

It is THIS cancer

which is the **most**

deadly of all cancers

for MEN.

85

Now what!?!

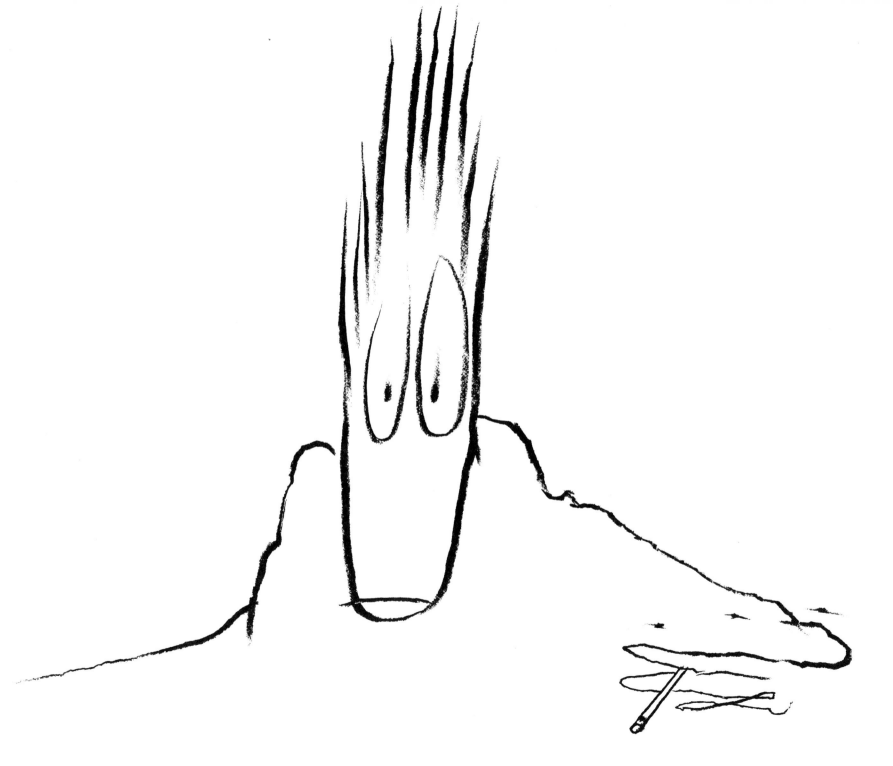

Simply this:

the <u>MORE</u> you inhale . . .

the greater your chances of having one,

or every one, of the ill effects of smoking:

1. the slow destruction of your lungs

2. cancer

3. the stomach troubles

4. the circulatory troubles of blood vessels and heart.

These are the demonstrated and DEPRESSING facts.

But HOW to stop?

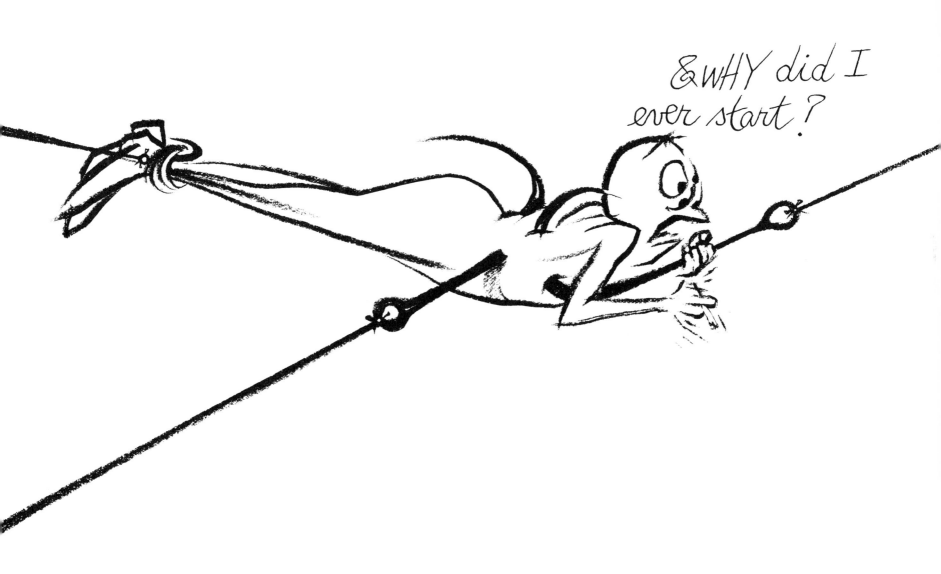

Ask any older person who smokes

whether he or she would start now.

Here's how:

How to STOP

YOU must truly WANT to stop

—and no self-deception on this point!

(If you're not sure you can do it by yourself and need help,

see your doctor or join an anti-smoking clinic)

Don't try to stop

SUDDENLY

and dramatically

before you're prepared.

It won't work.

Recognize that you are

dealing with a HABIT.

The fight is going to be to DESTROY

it and evaporate it.

PREPARE your conscious self and

your subconscious. Tell yourself by day,

"I am going to STOP smoking."

Also say it to yourself just before

you go to sleep.

Understand WHY you are stopping

and what you'll gain from stopping.

Then pick the RIGHT day

(NOT a time of meetings or parties

or stress)

and then QUIT!

Launch yourself with

as much MOMENTUM

and initiative

as possible.

This makes the first trials easier.

MOST

DON'T MAKE A

One puff reinforces the old habit and GREATLY injures

your next attempt to stop. It's as though

you were winding up a ball of yarn and kept dropping it.

When you foresee times coming which were favorite smoking

times, brace for them. Tell yourself,

"I'm not going to give in!"

IMPORTANT!
SINGLE EXCEPTION!

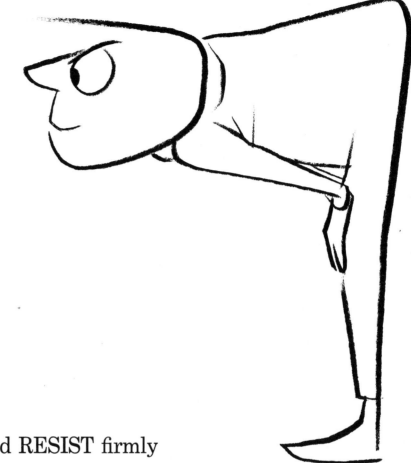

And whenever you're tempted RESIST firmly

for a minute and the worst of the desire will pass.

Do all sorts of other things for the first five days but DON'T smoke.

Avoid meetings and people that tempt you to smoke!

When the worst of the withdrawal is over, begin

to reinforce your NEW habit by "workouts"

in fighting the old habit. Watch other smokers.

Smell the smoke of someone else's pipe or cigarette.

"But never suffer an exception to occur 'till the new habit is securely rooted in your life."

—William James

Pamper yourself!

Life Savers, mints, gum, crack

and eat nuts, noisy celery,

take hot baths, eat foods you LIKE.

Go on a fruit jag.

The smell
of VICTORY!

At last! No more puffing and shortness of breath.

No more $100 burned each year.

After 6 months no more "smoker's cough."

Your digestion is clearly improving.

BOTH hands are free again and you don't

have to carry the equipment any more.

Your taste is returning.

And so is the strong and highly enjoyable sense of SMELL.

Above all you FEEL better. You have a NEW ENERGY.

You've got the tars and the nicotines off your back.

YOU ARE FREE!

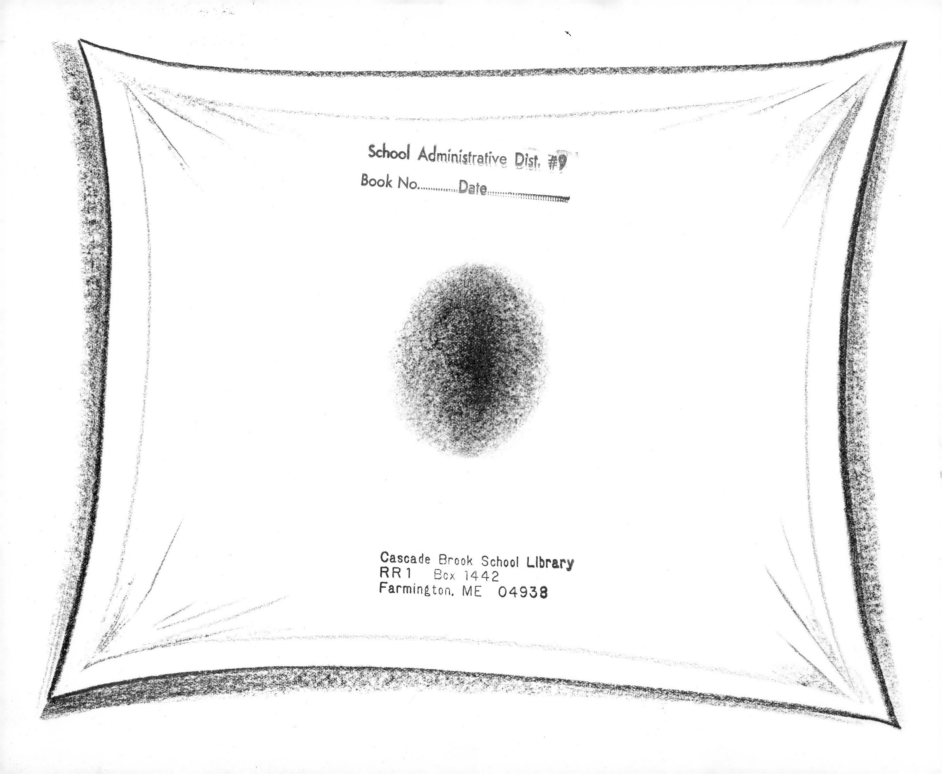